STARTER PLACES

Greece

Macdonald Educational

About Starters Places

Starters Places provide an entertaining and informative introduction for young children to various countries and their national characteristics.

The vocabulary is controlled for reading by young children, and about 90 per cent of the words in the book should be familiar to young readers.

Each book contains material for further activities and research, such as an easy reference map, a table of simple facts, a project, a dictionary and an index.

Teachers and experts have been consulted on the content and accuracy of the books.

Illustrated by: Margaret Belsky

Written and planned by: Sandie Oram

Managing editor: Su Swallow

Editorial assistant: Diana Darley

Production: Stephen Pawley, Rosemary Bishop

Art consultant: Geoffrey Dickinson of *Punch*

Reading consultant: Donald Moyle, author of *The Teaching of Reading* and senior lecturer in education at Edge Hill College of Education

Chairman, teacher advisory panel: F. F. Blackwell, Director, Primary Extension Programme, National Council for Educational Technology; general inspector for schools (primary), London Borough of Croydon

Teacher panel: Loveday Harmer, Lynda Snowdon, Joy West, Enid Wilkinson

Colour reproduction by
Colourcraftsmen Limited

ISBN 0 356 04319 3
Made and printed in England by
Hazell Watson & Viney Ltd
Aylesbury, Buckinghamshire

Filmset by
Layton-Sun Limited

First published 1973 by
Macdonald and Company
(Publishers) Limited
St. Giles House
49-50 Poland Street
London W1

These people are in a Greek taverna.
They are choosing their dinner
in the kitchen.
They point to the food they want.

Now their dinner is ready.
They sit down and eat it.
They watch a Greek dance
while they are eating.

Here is the theatre at Epidaurus.
This theatre is very old.
It is in the open air.
But everyone can hear the actors.

Greece has many old buildings.
The Parthenon is the most famous.
People from all over the world
come to see these ruins.

These tourists are buying presents
to take home with them.
They can have their shoes shined.

Tourists often buy Greek rugs.
These women are making a rug.
One woman is spinning the wool.
The other is weaving the rug.

These people have come to buy some pots.
They watch the potter at his wheel.

Here are some divers.
They are diving for sponges.
They hang the sponges up to dry.

There are many Greek islands.
People can visit the islands by boat.

The Greek navy has a festival
every year.
People come to see the big ships
in the harbour.

Many famous shipowners live in Greece.
Some of their ships are built in Greece.
Some are built in other countries.

Many people come to Greece
on holiday.
Some go to the island of Mykonos.
Mykonos has windmills on the hills.

Many parts of Greece are very hilly.
People travel on mules
up the rocky paths.
This family is moving house.

Many Greek people own small farms.
These farmers keep bees.
The bees make honey.

The farmers keep goats too. The farmer's wife makes yoghourt from goats' milk.

Other Greek farmers grow grapes.
They dry the grapes in the sun.
The dried grapes are called raisins.

These people have just picked
all the olives.
Now they are having a festival.

It is Good Friday.
These people are in
an Easter procession.

Here are some Greek soldiers.
They are called evzones.
They are wearing uniform.

Greece long ago

Long ago the first Olympic games were held in Greece.
The pictures show some of the athletes.

Greeks used many statues
to decorate streets and buildings.
This sculptor is carving a statue.

These men are leaping over a bull.
The King of Crete came to watch them.

Some Greek monks built their monasteries high up in the mountains.
They needed ladders to climb up.
Some were lifted up in baskets.

1. Heat 2 pints of milk.
   Do not let it boil.

2. Stir in a carton
   of plain yoghourt.

3. Pour into glasses
   on a tray.
   Cover the glasses
   with a towel.

4. Leave in the airing cupboard
   for 6 hours.

You can make a lot of yoghourt
for your friends.
You need a carton of yoghourt
and some milk.

Starter's **Greek** words

Greece is Ἑγγὰς
taverna is ταβέρνα
theatre is θέατρο
rug is τάπης
sponge is σπόγγος
windmill is ἀνεμόμυλος
mule is μουλάρι
honey is μέλι
yoghourt is γιαούρτι
raisins is σταφίδες
olives is ἐλιές

Here are some Greek words.
They are written in the Greek alphabet.
The Greek alphabet is different
from ours.

Index